Following Jesus on Mission Together

Devotional and Journal

Contents

GettingStarted... 05
Retreat & Advance....................................... 07

Prepare:... 09
Day 1   Teach Us to Pray....................... 10
Day 2   Our Father................................. 12
Day 3   Your Father the King.................. 14
Day 4   Your Father Provides.................. 16
Day 5   Your Father Forgives.................. 18
Day 6   Your Father Guides..................... 20
Day 7   Your Father Protects................... 22

Present:... 24
Day 1   Sent Ones................................. 26
Day 2   Spirit Power.............................. 28
Day 3   Be a Branch.............................. 30
Day 4   Called to Relationship................ 32
Day 5   Go to the Cross........................ 34
Day 6   The Jesus Way......................... 36
Day 7   Listen like Jesus....................... 38
Day 8   Give Thanks............................. 40
Day 9   Encourage................................ 42
Day 10   Praise...................................... 44

Reflect and Respond:................................. 46
Debrief and Share... 48

Getting Started

"But you will receive power when the Holy Spirit comes on you; and you will be my witnesses in Jerusalem, and in all Judea and Samaria, and to the ends of the earth."
Jesus to His followers in Acts 1:8

This little book is a tool to assist you as you prepare to follow Jesus into a different cultural context. Each day there is Scripture and some brief devotional thoughts. On corresponding pages there is space to respond through journaling. In addition, there are some helpful tools at the end of this book.

The first part (Prepare) walks you through the movements and truths found in the Lord's Prayer. Begin this section one week before you leave, to prepare your heart. The second part (Present) is a daily journey of key missional insights from Scripture while you are present in a different cultural context. The third part (Reflect and Respond) is a short debrief tool to use on one of your final days before you go. This will assist you in considering how God has gotten your attention through the experience, what He is saying to you, and what you will do about it.

The heart behind this book is to assist you in listening and learning from God and the people you encounter (revelation) so that you can faithfully respond.
God is already present and working among the people you will be building relationships with. Jesus said, *"My Father is always at His work to this very day, and I too am working."* - *John 5:17*. Therefore, the good news is that you don't have to fit God into your luggage and bring Him with you. He is already there and doing His thing.

Retreat and Advance

"Very early in the morning, while it was still dark, Jesus got up, left the house and went off to a solitary place, where He prayed." - Mark 1:35

"But Jesus often withdrew to lonely places and prayed." - Luke 5:16

"One of those days Jesus went out to a mountainside to pray, and spent the night praying to God." - Luke 6:12

As we look at the story of Jesus we recognize that He regularly had a pattern of retreating with His Father God and then advancing in His Father's work. This is the way of Jesus and therefore, it will set the pattern for this experience. After all, if Jesus recognized His need to be with His Father, how much more do we need life giving time with Him? It is in times of retreat that we remember who God is and who we are. It is in these times of pulling away that we can receive revelation and begin to recognize what God is wanting to say and show us. Retreat is an invitation to enjoy God and be empowered by Him to join His Kingdom work around us.

Therefore, make it a priority to retreat and advance in this journey. Retreat through the devotional, through prayer, and journaling. Then be sent out responding to the revelation God has provided you.

So, let's get started!

Prepare

"Your Word is a lamp to guide my feet and a light for my path." - Psalm 119:105

Begin this section one week prior to your travel day to set your vision and attention on God and His Kingdom. We will be focusing on an element from the Lord's Prayer each day as we lean into our relationship with God. Mike Breen writes in his book "Building a Discipleship Culture" about the importance of the Lord's Prayer saying, *"Thus, when Jesus is teaching His followers to pray, He is showing them how to walk with God. If walking with God truly is what our lives are all about, praying the way Jesus shows us is a major part of our life."* May this familiar prayer nourish your soul and prepare you to follow Jesus on His mission with others.

Let's prayerfully read the prayer of Jesus:
"Our Father in heaven,
hallowed be Your name,
Your kingdom come,
Your will be done,
*   on earth as it is in heaven.*
Give us today our daily bread.
And forgive us our debts,
*   as we also have forgiven our debtors.*
And lead us not into temptation,
*   but deliver us from the evil one."*
- Matthew 6:9-13

Day 1 :: Teach Us to Pray   Date:

"One day Jesus was praying in a certain place. When He finished, one of His disciples said to Him, "Lord, teach us to pray, just as John taught his disciples." - Luke 11:1

Prayer was a regular rhythm of life for Jesus and so His disciples were able to observe and hear His prayers. Jesus' followers wanted to pray like Jesus. What was it about the prayers of Jesus that caused His followers to desire to pray like Him? What do you think?

Whatever the reason, one of Jesus' disciples asked Jesus how they should pray. I love the hunger and humility in the words of this disciple: *"Lord, teach us to pray."* It reminds me of the movie "Gravity." In this survival story set in the harsh environment of space, the main character is a woman named Dr. Ryan Stone. In an emotional scene she remarks that she'd pray for herself, but she had never prayed in her life. Then she explains, *"Nobody ever taught me how."* It was a painful and lonely statement.

As we begin this journey we want to begin with humility, with hope, and a hunger to encounter God. Therefore, let's join Jesus' first disciples in asking: *"King Jesus, please teach me to pray."* Prayer is a conversation with God that shapes us, changes things around us, and connects us with our loving heavenly Father. Therefore, we want to pray and follow the way of Jesus and reflect on the prayer of Jesus.

How is God getting your attention?

Day 2 :: Our Father   Date:

"Our Father in heaven, hallowed be Your name," - Matt.6:9

Jesus leads us to address God as Father. There are a lot of ways we could refer to God, but Jesus encourages us to begin by seeing God as our loving heavenly Father. Therefore, if we are to approach God as a father, it means we are His beloved children.

In Matthew 7, Jesus encourages His followers to persist in prayer and then in verse 11 He explains, *"If you, then, though you are evil, know how to give good gifts to your children, how much more will your Father in heaven give good gifts to those who ask Him!"*

God is a good, present, and powerful Father who listens, provides, protects, leads, and walks with us. God is a loving Dad that gives good gifts to the children He cares for deeply. So, Jesus revealed that we first come near to God in prayer as His child. What an amazing way to begin prayer!

Does your prayer life have a sense of closeness to God?
How do you tend to imagine God?
How does the truth of you being God's beloved child shape how you think about joining God on mission?

How is God getting your attention?

Day 3 :: Your Father the King   Date:

"Your Kingdom come, Your will be done, on earth as it is in heaven." - Matt.6:10

Jesus makes it clear that we are God's beloved children and He is our good Father. But, our Heavenly Father is also the King of all things. Therefore, Jesus teaches us to pray for God's rule and reign to be a reality more and more here like it is in heaven.

When we recognize that our Father is THE King of ALL and we ask Him to have His will done among us, we are humbly setting aside our agenda and need to be in control. When we pray for God's Kingdom to come, we are submitting ourself to God, to His plans, purposes, and to His ways of doing things.

As you prepare to travel and meet new people in a new place, keep this line of the prayer in front of you. When you do, it can become a prompt to watch for where God is already at work around you and it cultivates a spirit of humility and trust in God.

What is your response to your Father God being the King of ALL?

How could regularly praying this line of the prayer before you go and during your trip impact you?

How is God getting your attention?

Day 4 :: Your Father the Provider   Date:

"Give us today our daily bread." - Matt.6:11

Jesus invites us to bring our daily needs to our Father God and to recognize that He is our good and faithful provider. We all have needs. These needs range from physical, emotional, spiritual, financial, relational, and intellectual needs. God is our good Father who can provide for all of our needs and Jesus encourages us to ask and depend on Him.

Are you good at asking for help? Many times people struggle to ask for help. Maybe it's because they fear it looks like weakness or somehow reflects poorly on them. Perhaps they have a hard time asking for help because they are ashamed or don't want to inconvenience someone else. The good news is that Jesus encourages us to bring even our smallest most basic need (daily bread) to God and to ask Him for provision.

As you prepare to go and join your team in this experience you will find yourself in need. Maybe you have financial needs right now. Perhaps you will have physical challenges on your journey. It could be that you will have some emotionally stretching times. Bring your needs to God, no matter the size and ask for help from those around you.

What do you need right now? Where do you lack?

How is God getting your attention?

Day 5 :: Your Father Forgives   Date:

"And forgive us our debts, as we also have forgiven our debtors." - Matt.6:12

We all sin and we all hurt one another. The good news is that God forgives. In 1 John 1:9 it tells us that, *"If we confess our sins, He is faithful and just and will forgive us our sins and purify us from all unrighteousness."* The confession part can be sticky. We may not like to admit when we blow it, but when we bring our failures, sins, and wrong-doing into the light we find God's gracious forgiveness.

Forgiveness is something we need to receive and give. But, sometimes it can be easier to offer grace and understanding for ourselves, but not for those around us. Yet in this prayer Jesus invites us to forgive others as we also personally seek God's forgiveness. While you are on this trip you may find yourself in need of offering and receiving forgiveness from those around you. Let us follow the way of Jesus and forgive one another as we seek God's forgiveness in our own lives.

Forgiveness is a choice. Here is a helpful tool to use:

"God, I choose to forgive _____, even though they _____, which made me feel _____. Amen."

How is God getting your attention?

Is God nudging you to forgive someone?

Day 6 :: Your Father Guides   Date:

"And lead us not into temptation," - Matt.6:13

Jesus is encouraging us to pray that God would lead us and guide us so that we might be faithful to Him in our world. God is a Father who doesn't just drop us off to figure out life on our own. He desires to walk before us, to lead us, and guide us. In fact, often God is described as a shepherd and His people are described as His flock following His lead and depending on His protection and provision. On one occasion Jesus referred to Himself as the Good Shepherd and stated that His followers are His sheep. He said, *"My sheep listen to my voice; I know them, and they follow me" (John 10:27).*

That is a powerful promise. Let's read that again. But before we do. Read it like it is true and like you believe it.

"My sheep listen to my voice; I know them, and they follow me." - Jesus in John 10:27

Here is the truth that pops out at me for us today:
Jesus is speaking to you.
You can know Jesus' voice.
Jesus knows you.
You can follow Him.

This trip will be a moment to quiet the noise around you and to listen to God and follow. What is He saying to you?

How is God getting your attention?

Day 7 :: Your Father Protects   Date:

"...but deliver us from the evil one." - Matt.6:13

Jesus sent His followers out into battle and He went first. In Acts 10:38, Jesus' friend Peter gave a great description of Jesus' ministry. He stated, you know how *"God anointed Jesus of Nazareth with the Holy Spirit and power, and how He went around doing good and healing all who were under the power of the devil, because God was with Him."* Jesus was empowered by the Holy Spirit and pushed back against the work of the devil.

Spiritual warfare is real and so Jesus encourages us to pray for victory in the battle. The good news is that Jesus has already told us that there will be victory.

Another helpful passage is James 4:7-8 that encourages us to *"Submit yourselves, then, to God. Resist the devil, and he will flee from you. Come near to God and He will come near to you."* The focus is not on the evil one and being preoccupied with him, but on getting close to God and following His lead.

One of the greatest weapons we can use in the spiritual battle we are in is prayer. Prayer is not merely preparation for the battle - it is the battle. So let us pray on the spot, on location, in every circumstance, in times of anxiety, in times of joy, and ask for God to do what only He can.

How is God getting your attention?

Present

"The Word (speaking of Jesus) became flesh and made His dwelling among us. We have seen His glory, the glory of the one and only Son, who came from the Father, full of grace and truth."
- John 1:14

Begin this section on the day of your arrival. In this journey, you are following the way of Jesus. In the passage above, we recognize that Jesus was a missionary and became present with us. His presence among us was marked by grace and truth.

Jesus once called Himself the way, the truth, and the life (John 14:6). Jesus is our way to life and He is to be our way of life. Therefore, we want to learn how to join God's beautiful Kingdom mission like Jesus did. Therefore, this section will provide daily devotional thoughts to help you follow the way of Jesus, reflection questions, journaling space, and helpful insights to being present in new contexts.

Before you turn the page and begin your journey, here is a prayer promise from Joshua 1:9 for you.

"Have I not commanded you? Be strong and courageous. Do not be afraid; do not be discouraged, for the Lord your God will be with you wherever you go." - Joshua 1:9

Day 1 :: Sent Ones   Date:

"'Peace be with you! As the Father has sent me, I am sending you.' And with that He breathed on them and said, 'Receive the Holy Spirit.'" - Jesus in John 20:21-22

After Jesus was resurrected from the dead He appeared to His followers and called them to join His mission. He started by saying, "as the Father has sent me…"

How did God the Father send Jesus?

Jesus was sent to us and became one of us. He moved into our neighborhood and entered into our mess. He did good, healed the sick, made disciples, proclaimed God's truth, showed God's love, served and gave His life. He saw what God was doing in the world around Him and He joined in God's mission.

Jesus is saying to His followers - including you, "I was sent this way by my Father God to be a missionary and so now I'm sending you to be like me and do what I did - to join in God's mission - just like I did. Jesus, the first missionary, challenges us to be a missionary ("sent one") like Him.

If you are a "sent one" - then who is the one sending you?

What is their hope and desire for you, for your team members, and those you are visiting?

Take a moment and begin to ask God to show you where He is already at work around you so you can join in.

Day 2 :: Spirit Power   Date:

"'Peace be with you! As the Father has sent me, I am sending you.' And with that He breathed on them and said, 'Receive the Holy Spirit.'" - Jesus in John 20:21-22

Jesus called His followers to be missionaries like Him, but He also sought to empower them with the Holy Spirit like He was. Therefore, we see Jesus saying, *"receive the Holy Spirit."* Later, Jesus made it clear that His followers were not to go and jump into mission until they had received power from the presence of the Holy Spirit (Acts 1:4). He went on to declare, *"But you will receive power when the Holy Spirit comes on you; and you will be my witnesses in Jerusalem, and in all Judea and Samaria, and to the ends of the earth." (Acts 1:8)*

Jesus accomplished His mission in the power of the Holy Spirit and promised to send the same Spirit to live in you and empower you.

In Luke 11 Jesus promised that God was a good Father who gives His Spirit to His children who ask. Consider asking for a fresh filling of God's Spirit even now.

Where do you sense that you need God's presence and power most on this trip?

Again, take a moment and begin to ask the Holy Spirit to show you where God is already at work around you so you can join in.

Day 3 :: Be a Branch   Date:

"I am the vine; you are the branches. If you remain in me and I in you, you will bear much fruit; apart from me you can do nothing." - Jesus to His followers in John 15:5

Jesus had a fruitful life and accomplished incredible things and He wanted His followers to be fruitful as well. Therefore, Jesus knew His followers would need to learn His pattern of life of retreating with His Father God in relationship and then advancing with His Father God on mission. Jesus spent time remaining close to God and from that place would live a fruitful life. Jesus knows that we can sometimes try to take on all the responsibility to make things happen and forget that real change and fruit happens because of Him. He is the vine and we are the branch. Life comes from Him, so we have to stay connected to Him. Remember, Jesus said that apart from Him we can do nothing. That is freeing! But, it also is a call to prioritize connecting with Jesus, to listen to Him, and develop a closeness to Him. When we do, we grow and follow His lead, and step out in faith and God gives us opportunities to join His fruitful work around us.

What you are doing right now is a part of learning to remain and stay connected with Jesus.

What do you think is the fruit (the Jesus Kingdom results) that God would desire for this trip?

Consider taking some time to write out an honest prayer to God about wherever you are at right now. Just be real and know He cares. Perhaps take a moment and quietly listen to see if He has anything He'd like to say to you and write it down.

Day 4 :: Called to Relationship   Date:

"'Come, follow me,' Jesus said, 'and I will send you out to fish for people.' - Jesus to His followers in Mark 1:17

Jesus invited His followers to literally follow after Him. He was inviting them to become His student and to be with Him and to learn to become like Him. He called them into a relationship. So, Jesus' followers spent the next few years being with Jesus and learning to follow His way of life. To follow Jesus is to enter into a relationship.

You are on a journey right now with other people. In addition, you are interacting with folks in the place God has put you for this moment. Most likely you have tasks to accomplish, but remember that relationship comes first. This is where Jesus began and it's from this place that true lasting change takes place. Yes, seek to accomplish the tasks around you. But, give your first and best investment to your relationships with God, with your team members, and with your partners.

Some of us are a bit more quiet and others of us are more outgoing. That's fine. Recognize that God has placed you on this team for a reason. You are a gift! Take another step into relationship with someone around you today - in your own way.

What has been a difficult thing about connecting with team members or the people in the place you are in?

What have been some life-giving relationships so far in this journey? Why?

How can you invest in one particular relationship today?

Day 5 :: Go to the Cross   Date:

"Then He said to the crowd, "If any of you wants to be my follower, you must give up your own way, take up your cross daily, and follow me. If you try to hang on to your life, you will lose it. But if you give up your life for my sake, you will save it." - Jesus in Luke 9:23-24

To follow Jesus is to follow Him to the cross, to die to ourselves, and to be raised to new life. This is the journey of trusting God, finding joy, and surrender. It can be difficult, painful, but life changing.

Take a moment and look at the cross illustration below.

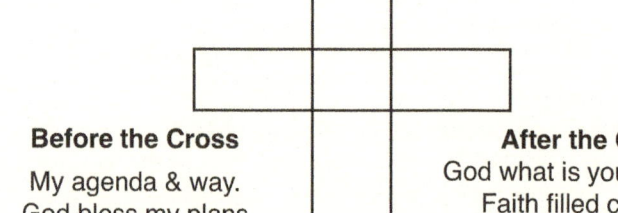

Before the Cross
My agenda & way.
God bless my plans.
Live for myself.
Seek to control.
Choose comfort over all.
Little need for trust.

After the Cross
God what is your agenda?
Faith filled courage.
Contentment.
Power and peace.
New life and Blessing.
Submitted to God.

On the Cross
Confess and Repent.
Die to self and surrender.
Give God our agenda and control.
Give God the results and expectations.
Battle, brokenness, pressure, and pain.

What do you sense God inviting you to put on the cross? Are you open? Why or why not?

How is God getting your attention today?

Day 6 :: The Jesus Way   Date:

"Then make me truly happy by agreeing wholeheartedly with each other, loving one another, and working together with one mind and purpose.

Don't be selfish; don't try to impress others. Be humble, thinking of others as better than yourselves. Don't look out only for your own interests, but take an interest in others, too.

You must have the same attitude that Christ Jesus had. Though He was God, He did not think of equality with God as something to cling to.

Instead, He gave up His divine privileges; He took the humble position of a slave and was born as a human being.

When He appeared in human form, He humbled Himself in obedience to God and died a criminal's death on a cross."
- Philippians 2:2-8

The Scripture above tells us that when Jesus came to us, He set aside His own divine advantages and rights and took the form of a servant. He came to serve, not be served. Jesus invites us to follow His way of life.

Take some time and read through the passage above a couple times and circle or underline any words or phrases that God may be highlighting for you.

Why do you think God is bringing that word or phrase to mind?

How will you practically respond to how God has gotten your attention today?

Day 7 :: Listen like Jesus   Date:

Jesus was walking and a man who was blind yelled to get Jesus' attention. Jesus went over to the man and had this interaction with him:

"What do you want me to do for you?" Jesus asked.
"My Rabbi," the blind man said, "I want to see!"
- Mark 10:51

Then Jesus healed the man of his blindness.

The man was blind! Why did Jesus ask him what he wanted? Isn't it obvious?

We may find ourselves in a situation where we believe the fix and the next step is obvious. But, Jesus gives us a great pattern to follow in this story. When we enter a new place we go with humble hearts and our ears open to listen and learn. We may think we have the "right" way to do something, but in reality it may just be a different way and we miss the opportunity to grow as a result. Or, in our desire to help others, we might assume what is needed, but it's always best to follow the way of Jesus and humbly listen and learn first.

What is something you have learned while on your trip?

What needs have you heard from your team?

What needs have you heard from the people you are visiting?

How will you practically respond to those needs today?

Day 8 :: Give Thanks   Date:

"Enter His gates with thanksgiving;
go into His courts with praise.
Give thanks to Him and praise His name.
For the Lord is good.
His unfailing love continues forever,
and His faithfulness continues to each generation."
- Psalm 100:4-5

This Psalm encourages us to enter God's presence by first giving thanks to God. Giving thanks is a wonderful way to worship God and acknowledge what He has done.

Giving thanks is also a helpful way to push back against times when we are feeling discontent, negative, and wishing things were different.

Today let us live out 1 Thessalonians 5:18 that says, *"Be thankful in all circumstances, for this is God's will for you who belong to Christ Jesus."*

Take some time today and write down what you are thankful for…

About God

During this trip

In your life

How is God getting your attention?

Day 9 :: Encourage   Date:

Therefore encourage one another and build each other up, just as in fact you are doing.
- 1 Thessalonians 5:11

"But encourage one another daily, as long as it is called "Today," so that none of you may be hardened by sin's deceitfulness."   *- Hebrews 3:13*

To encourage someone is come alongside them so you can give them courage. Encouragement delivers strength, comfort, and builds others up. Sometimes encouragement challenges people in love.

The image that comes to mind are the friends of a fifth grade student who finds himself frozen in fear at the top of high ropes course. The friends encourage their buddy and cheer for him. They seek to fill him with courage while letting him know he is not alone.

Who in your life has been an encourager?
What has made them so encouraging?

Who is God bringing to mind that you can encourage today? How?

How is God getting your attention?

Day 10 :: Praise   Date:

"Praise the Lord!
Praise the Lord from heaven!
Praise God on the heights!
Praise God, all of you who are his messengers!
Praise God, all of you who comprise his heavenly forces!
Sun and moon, praise God!
All of you bright stars, praise God!
You highest heaven, praise God!
Do the same, you waters that are above the sky!

Let all of these praise the Lord's name because God gave the command and they were created!" - Psalm 148:1-5

Pride says, "Look at me!"
Praise says, "Look at God!"

Praise responds to what God has done.

We close out our devotionals with an opportunity to give God praise for what He has done and who He is.

Put together a praise prayer/poem/song/drawing:
Here are some starter ideas…

I praise you God for… (what has God done?)

Praise God in… (name places or landscapes of where you've been)

I praise you God for being… (who has God revealed Himself to be?)

Reflect and Respond

"Anyone who listens to my teaching and follows it is wise, like a person who builds a house on solid rock."
- Jesus in Matthew 7:24

This section is for your debriefing time with your team. The goal is to help you identify how God has been speaking to you through this experience and how you can respond.

Layout of Next Steps:
First, take a moment and ask God to speak to you and give you clarity as you reflect on the experience you've had.

Second, look over your journal notes and think back on the time you've spent and what you did each day. Remember significant moments, conversations, or experiences.

Third, take time to answer the questions on the next couple pages. Some are fun and light-hearted and others more meaningful.

Then, you will get together with your team to talk through the questions and process the trip together.

Debrief Questions   Date:

What did you like best about the trip?

What did you learn about the country and people you visited?

What was something about the culture that you really enjoyed and will miss? What is something that was difficult for you?

What words would you use to describe the people you visited? Is there any person in particular that you had a special connection with?

What was something that surprised you or you didn't expect?

What was the most difficult or disappointing thing for you?

What was something you learned about God on this trip? Or, where did you see God at work?

How has God gotten your attention through this time?
What is God saying to you?
What will you do about it?